To My Auntie Che

Love you for u

May God continue

to bless

Love
E

THE ART OF BOUNCING BACK

HOW I SURVIVED IT ALL

EBONY K. JOHNSON

THE ART OF BOUNCING BACK: HOW I SURVIVED IT ALL

Copyright © 2017 by Ebony K. Johnson, Ambitionz R Us, LLC

All right reserved. No parts of this book may be reproduced or transmitted in any form or by any means, electronic or mechanical, including photocopying, recording, or by any information storage and retrieval system, without written permission from the author, accept for inclusion of brief quotations in a review.

ISBN-13: 978-0692818886 (Ambitionz R Us Publishing)

ISBN-10: 069281888X

Printed in the United States of America

Unless otherwise indicated, reference from How to Go On Living When Someone You Love Dies. By: Therese A Rondo, Ph.D. Copyright © 1988

This book recounts events in the life of Ebony K. Johnson per the author's recollection and perspective. While all stories are, true identifying details have been changed to protect the privacy of those involved.

For more information contact:
Website: www.ambitionzrus.com
Email: EbonyKJohnson@ambitionzrus.com

"IN LOVING MEMORY OF..."

My Great Grandmother Mildred "Mershaw" Green, the greatest lesson you blessed me with was the art of making something out of nothing and for that I am forever grateful.

&

My Brother Andre "Dre" Moore, through your life and your death has taught me great strength, perseverance, and self-reliance

I Love You

Table of Contents

Dedication……………………………………………….8

Why Did I Write This Book?................................14

INTRODUCTION……………………………………..17

Bounce Back 1: Shhh I Have Secrets!..................20

Bounce Back 2: I Dated Death…………………….42

Bounce Back 3: The Birth of The Over Achiever…………52

Bounce Back 4: A Father's Betrayal………………….57

Bounce Back 5: The Healing…………………………72

Bounce Back 6: What Are Your Pearls?................78

My Final Thoughts…………………………………….81

About Author…………………………………………..83

BE THE PERSON WHO can BOUNCE BACK FROM ANY SITUATION WITH GRACE~

EBONY K. JOHNSON

Dedication

I dedicate this book to; those who have experienced many storms in life. You may have come out battered, bruised, maybe a little broken, and with a few scares but baby please don't ever give up on you because God never gave up you.

To all those daughters who fathers have abandoned them or they are not man enough to care for them; honey please know that you are not your father's mistake. Believe that you hold the love required within and it should never be dependent upon another person's actions.

To the beautiful women who thought they were unworthy of love; never let the insecurities of others projected towards you dim the light God has placed over your crown of greatness.

I thank God for giving me unshakable faith, a logical mind, a big heart, and a sense of calm that I longed for. The most High has definitely saved me from myself and the dangers of this cold world. Thank God, every storm that tried to break me because with each shock of lighting I felt penetrate my body, I could hear God telling me never to give up or give in. With each lesson acquired while speaking my mantra "Girllllll, conquer and defeat that ish" I faced any obstacle it allowed me to master the art of bouncing back no matter the hand I was dealt.

I would like to thank my mother, Eunice Johnson, for her love, support, and trust in me no matter how crazy my ideas were or continue to be.

I would like to thank my brother, Andre Moore, for the years we had together, our many sibling fights, and the strength you give me from heaven.

To my nephew, Kedric Green, you have been the motivation behind so much of my grind since the day you were born always know that I believe in you.

To my grandmother, Roselee Moore, thank you for your many prayers, calm conversations, and putting me on your Dr. Granny couch (a.k.a. Dr. Phil couch).

To my big cousin/big sister, Elesha Bridgers, thank you for helping me get back to the light.

To my aunts, uncles, cousins, and my friends who have become family thank you for all your love and support I am eternally grateful.

To my mentors, coaches, protégés, and the many strangers I have met via social media who have been a major support system, I thank you from the depths of my heart. More importantly, thank you for taking this journey with me, purchasing my book, and mastering the art of bouncing back in your own lives.

Lastly, I would like to thank my father, Andre Johnson, and others like you, for underestimating me, showing me that life is not what it seems to be at times, and for not seeing my value. ~You tried to break me, belittle me, and destroy me, but God saw better for me.

These lessons have taught me my most valuable lesson to date; how to *Master The Art of Bouncing Back* while fully trusting in God throughout the process.

Ebony K. Johnson

I CHOOSE ME PLEDGE

I Choose Me Because I'm ROYALTY!

I Choose Me Because I'm WORTH IT!

I Choose Me Because I'm ENOUGH!

I Choose Me Because I'm GREATNESS!

I Choose Me Because _____!
                              (Fill in the blank)

Why Did I Write This Book?

I decided to write this book not only for my own healing, but for others facing similar difficulties. When I told people about my circumstances they always replied one of two ways, 'How the hell did you survive all of that?' they would ask, or they would comment that my story blessed their lives. Oddly enough, sometimes both responses were shared at the same darn time. My reply always came from a place of shame, anger, and embarrassment. I had no idea that my trials and tribulations in my life that brought me so much pain and shame would one day be a blessing to others just by surviving it all. What I thought was shameful and completely embarrassing had become a blessing to others who were experiencing or living through similar events was amazing to me. I thought I was the only one truly living a real freaking LifeTime Movie. Of course, right?

But, as I traveled through the valleys in my life, I felt like I was the only one on earth with these experiences. But, the truth is unfortunately, I was not alone. I was just bold enough to speak on it even when every fear-seeking bone in my body screamed what the HELL are you doing exposing us woman? Are you insane? Yet, I know when God is moving in my life and He has an assignment for me, I am unable to sleep peacefully until I am obedient to His direction.

I had many signs and people urging me to write about my story. It wasn't until I was still and had a long, hard, stern conversation with God for a while, but mainly listened to what he placed on my heart. Again, like any scared shitless woman opening every old scar she could remember has added to the pure badass you see before you, I wanted to run in the other direction and join the witness protection program erasing all acknowledgment of my own history. But who was I kidding? I can't run from God! Even as my anxiety grew, so did my determination to conquer the fear and excuses that tried to evade my whole being. So, I quietly reminded myself 'if it was easy your journey would have not been worth it, beautiful'.

God continues to work on me, especially because your girl is super private. I had to keep reminding myself, girl this is not about you, but the strength God has given you to turn your pain into purpose.

While writing this book, I had the most eye opening 'ahhh moments; (in my Oprah voice) because I then realized, I had normalized all of my trauma. By normalizing my trauma, I felt less ashamed and I was completely disengaged from my emotions (protective mechanism of sorts, I suppose). Yet, it was slowly destroying me on the inside, because, I mean let's face it people, there is nothing natural about the course of events I had experienced (large amounts of death, sexual assault, betrayal, etc).

Even though most moments for me writing this book were very therapeutic it also took me on a spiritual journey of God's truth for my life thus far by allowing me to understand why it was important for me to turn my pain into purpose. Learning God's truth has given me the ability to understand the lessons in each moment I experienced no matter how hard they were. I had to get real honest with myself and acknowledge what others thought should have destroyed me had empowered me. Go figure! Shh, big secret, being vulnerable is not my best outfit you know.

Yet, God knew when he was shaping me in all my flaws; I would use my pain as a vessel to be a blessing to others just by sharing my story. Pain is an interesting emotion that has taken me down some dark paths, but God's light has always guided me when I would go astray.

As I expose the pain of my past, how I learned to be vulnerable in each moment, and how I learned to conquer and defeat fear with every stroke of the keyboard I regain parts of me back. I ask that as you turn the pages of my life - that you learn how to judge people less and truly get to know them more. Behind each person's eyes there is a story they are living (or have lived) that may have changed their lives forever (good or bad). Everyone has a story even you. Yes, life can be hard but never allow it to break you - *Master the Art of Bouncing Back*!

INTRODUCTION

Obstacles and challenges are part of our life, right? No matter how positive and successful you are, you will still face hardships in life. I can tell you that without challenges, I could not have learned the lessons I needed in my own life. We become smarter and stronger when we are left alone to deal with life's unexpected storms in hopes to strengthen ourselves as well as our relationship with God.

Now, don't get me wrong I am not here to preach to you but I can only tell you it was by the grace of God I am still alive to tell you my story in my right mind, with love in my heart, and relentless strength to never give up.

I have witnessed people talking endlessly about their problems rather than taking some serious action to correct them. We all know people who reside to dating their problems and for Pete's sake, even marrying them for eternity. They go on and on about the problematic situations instead of working on the solutions. If you meet such people after six months or a year, you will find them in similar circumstances, singing the same song, and placing blame on everyone but themselves. We know certain circumstances are not our fault exclusively, but we have wonderful ways of getting help, work on our healing, and building the determination to live a healthy productive life no matter what.

You are probably looking at this introduction, like Ebony girl, it is easier said than done. Yes, you are absolutely 100% correct! Even though the healing process has been very hard with continued challenges, I must admit it has been very liberating and I pray that it is for you as well. Ummmm yea, I can guarantee you that there are no shortcuts to this healing (I know you were thinking about it), but if you stay faithful to the process, you *will* see results.

How we deal with life challenges will vary from person to person. But, it is in those moments when most people feel dejected, upset, unloved, and helpless they often become the most creative and strongest. It is also in those moments that we find comfort in lovely words of inspiration and encouragement which strike our minds boosting our confidence to overcome those hard life challenges. The inspiration and encouragement that we get from our loved ones, friends, and even strangers during these times work as a tonic by inspiring us, like an angel, to move ahead with life. Inspiration, encouragement, and support provide us with a since of a nurturing environment that can help you discover your purpose through your pain.

The Art of Bouncing Back: How I Survived It All, is my journey which retells some of my life experiences through short stories to the best of my recollection. It is a love letter to that broken little girl who feels like because she's experienced trauma in life she's not meant to experience love as well. I pray my vulnerability helps others to release their own brokenness as you turn the pages of stories from my life. Some of the character names have been altered to protect myself and others. There are many moments that happen in our life time that we are not proud to scream from the mountain tops but I have chosen to highlight those moments that have truly shaped my life in ways I will try to describe. With interactive journaling sections within each chapter I pray you are open to participate and engage in your own healing as well if you have lived through similar life events.

Each journey is different. My prayer for you is that you will be able to take a small blueprint from each lesson, story, mistake, and storm I survived to know you can bounce back as well.

You may ask who am I to tell you how to bounce back in your life. I'm just a woman who has experienced life on a multitude of levels. I am not a licensed expert in the topics I will address, but I have taken the challenge of documenting my journey for those who have asked or have been wondering what it's like to fully throw yourself into the brutal but liberating moments that truly helped me bounce back from every situation I have faced so far.

I promise not to bore you to death with a lot of blah blah blah. You will learn and feel the emotion within my process of how I mastered *The Art of Bouncing Back* and how I truly survived it all.

The Art Of Bouncing Back: How I Survived it All!

Bounce Back 1:

Shhh…I Have Secrets!

Let's play house, Tammy told me as she began to lift my shirt. As I look perplexed not understanding the concept, she could see the discomfort on my face. Tammy was a much older girl but trusted by my family to baby sit me. I was around 8 or 9 at the time fully of life but torn between playing with my Barbie or playing football with the boys. Of course, I was a tomboy to the bone but a girly girl on some occasions. And on this day playing being girly was the pick of the day, so I thought!

She quickly whispered in my ear, it will be ok it's a fun game I was taught, it doesn't hurt, and it will make you feel good. But, as fast as she said that she also told me to not tell anyone about our little secret.

>Shhh…this is our little secret ok? As she looked at me scary.

>Ok, I guess. As I twiddled my fingers.

>You must do what I say, as she pointed down at me.

>Ummmmm, looking nervous

>I will be the daddy and you will be the mommy, she scolded.

>But you're a girl? As I nervously replied.

>That doesn't matter, just do it, she yelled.

As she pulled my pants down she tried to kiss me but I turned my head. She whispered again, don't forget you must do what I say because I am the daddy in this game. I said nothing as I laid there not understanding that I was being violated by Tammy who was just another little girl who had the same thing done to her it seems. With my pants, down below my knees, she lifted my shirt and began to touch my private parts in places only my mommy had taught me to wash. As she touched me, she said girl this is what daddy's like to do to mommies as she felt inside of my panties. My body did tingle just a little but I also felt very uncomfortable but Tammy was not done playing house with me. She asked me did I like it and I lied yes, but I was scared, very scared. My panties were the last thing she pulled down as she spread my legs open to lay on top of me moving up and down. As she started to remove herself from on top of me I thought to myself yes, we are finally done playing house and could play another game that was not so uncomfortable. But, we didn't she bent down and started to lick on my private parts. As I jumped and tried to push her off me but she pushed me down to continue. She would do that for a what seemed like forever until she just abruptly stopped and yelled at me to keep still as she inserted her fingers into my vagina roughly and hurting me. This went on for what seemed like an eternity. She finally stopped, with no words spoken just pointing to fix my clothes. I just sat there quiet, scared, confused, and waiting for either one of my parents to come save me from the babysitter.

  Once my mom came to pick me up I didn't speak a word I just rushed out to the car, but secretly I knew I was different after that day. I wanted to tell my mom or anyone but, I could hear Tammy whispering in my ear the whole entire ride home this is our little secret, right? At, that moment my voice was silenced. Which was odd for me because I was little miss chatter-box and proud of it. My mom had even gotten me the book to go with my nickname little miss chatter-box and even little miss bossy because honey I had that bossy thing down to a science. So, I thought!

My mother could not figure out why I did not want to be away from her much or stay the night at people houses at young age but my little secret had already taken its toll. Especially Tammy's house, I would never want to be left alone with her anymore. I would stay for a couple of hours, only while others were there, and never wanted to stay the night. I would always call my parent crying for someone to come and pick me up that very second. Sometimes they would come and get me and sometimes they wouldn't.

I was in the third grade my body had started to fill out and my bra size was a 36B. (Screaming) People did you hear me a freaking size 36B in the third grade. I was extremely tall for my age and I had started my period by the fifth grade, I was devastated.

Mommy I think im dying (shrugs shoulders)

Why do you think your dying? Mommy sounded puzzled.

I have blood in my panties and Im slowly dying.

Mommy mouth drops (silence)

Looking (mommy looks weird, am I really dying)

That's your period Ebony let show me how to use a

Maxie pad, mommy whispered.

Umm, no thank you mommy this will go away in a couple minutes, right?

No baby, you will have your cycle every month for about a week forever

I knew I was dying a slow death, now I really can't play football, especially with these two things growing on my chest.

Life was over as I knew for me by the fifth grade. I was awkwardly tall, with two footballs growing on my chest, and I was actively dying a slow death by bleeding every month for a whole week. I would hide in the bathroom when It was time to change my pad because I didn't want any of the other girls to know, it was awful. Oh, and boys were really starting to act weird around me as I questioned myself, could them smell me actively dying from the blood slowly draining out of my body? (as I looked around to make sure no one was staring at me).

Playing football was no longer fun and boys were starting to be gross. I was introduced to new games like hide and go freak, spin the bottle, and truth or dare. All the girls were playing the games in my neighborhood, it was the thing to do. Me the awkward tomboy had no idea how to play these game but, I quickly learned.

Ebony you must run and hide where a boy can find and you freak each other, Sarah stated.

How do you freak each other and why would I want him to find me? Looking grossed out.

Silly, it's when you pants rub with a boy and its fun that's why you let him find you, as Sarah laughed.

That gross, I screamed hesitantly. (but in the back of my mind it was like reliving what happen with Tammy all over again. But, I wanted to be cool).

Ok, count me in, I blurted out.

My first encounter with a boy playing hide and go freak, this idiot decided he want to do more than freak. The boy leaned in for a kiss and I hit him so hard he ran. Everyone teased me for days.

There went my notoriety for hide and go freak. Come to find out the boy really had a crush on me (go figure, even after I punched his lights out). I opted to play another round of hide and go freak and even the other games that involved kissing.

These activities carried me all the way through middle school. Once I entered middle school the game had changed and people were much more advanced than my-self. Good bye hide and go freak! Hello, sex education and I'm not talking about from my teachers. The girls around me were really doing the thing that I thought only grown-ups did. They were having real conversations about their sexual exploitations with their boyfriends who were already in high-school. I was still a virgin and had never experienced anything outside of hide and go freak with boys before. Of course, I had saw some adult HBO shows but never experienced the real thing before. Really? Like, who didn't' sneak and watch the adult shows once your parents went to bed. Shit, some nights I would stay up for hours looking and trying to figure out how some of those people could do some of the things they did. Don't judge me I was a very inquisitive young lady and even more so as an adult. (Laughs).

I was excited because boys, high-school boys were starting to take notice of me too. But, it was just one thing I was not experienced liked the girls at my school so I hope none of those boys are expecting anything from me. Or, were they?

New high-school boyfriend: hey shorty

Me: Hello

New high-school boyfriend: give me a kiss

Me: (sweating) umm ok – (inserts kiss, peck on the lips)

New high-school boyfriend: I mean a real kiss

Me: What the hell is a real kiss?

New high-school boyfriend: you know a little tongue action

It was in that moment my inexperience with boys had become noticeable and my new found high-school boyfriend was becoming annoyed by me. As we attempted to kiss with the tongue action in all, my mind would shift to the enormous amount of spit that was drooling from his mouth that made me want to throw up. Yup, kissing with all the tongue action was not my favorite past time.

Middle school had flown by and before I knew I was graduating the eighth grade and I would soon be on my way to high-school. It was the first day of summer and my high-school boyfriend had become very territorial especially when it was time for me to attend high-school as well. He had invited me over to his house to watch a movie as we did often. His demeanor was different this day and I had no idea my life was about to change. As we watched television he wanted to kiss as we often did which I despised the spit swapping and drooling on one another but he did, so I did it. He touches were more aggressive and his breathing was harder. I stopped him to finish watching the movie, which for the life of me I cannot remember the title of it. But, he wanted to continue kissing and having a spit fest. He began to unbutton my pants as he kissed me while sliding his hands down into my pants. As his actions changed I became paralyzed unable to move, talk, or utter my disdain for what was going on because it took me back to the moment as a child when Tammy wanted to play house. I froze and he asked?

High school boyfriend: you ok?

Me: I lied and whispered yes.

Let's face it I was a tomboy with a guy who was in high-school who love me right. He was popular, a fine specimen of chocolate goodness, and I really did believe he loved me. Honey, I did not want my high-school boyfriend to stop liking me so I let him continue without complaint. We went back to kissing with the tongue action as he undid my pants even more. He took my hand to feel on his penis and that was the first time I had felt one outside of pants rubbing playing hide and go freak, Chile it didn't feel like that at all. His penis was hard a rock and I had no idea why. Was is broken? Had it become deformed? What the hell was wrong with him? I was too scared to ask especially because he was breathing all hard like he was ready to an asthma attack or something. I should know, I had a couple of them in my day. Maybe he needed an ambulance?

    The spit swapping continued while he pulled my breast out of my bra then beginning to suck on them. I felt a feeling I had never experienced before. Besides, I was super happy to stop spit swapping and the drooling fest for what seemed like hours. He made his move and fully removed my pants and panties all in one swipe. Damn, that boy was fast with it. He whipped his penis, removed his pants, placed plastic on it, and got on top of me. It was different from how the traditional pants rubbing went but then I remembered from the HBO shows I snuck a watched the shit was about to go down. Just as the thought flashed through my mind so did excruciating pain (him trying to insert his manhood into my undiscovered territory) as he yelled you're a damn virgin, man what the f***. He stopped asking me was I ok? Again, I meekly replied yes but inside I was hurting. He continued slowly reinserting what I thought was his deformity which seemed like a couple of minutes of moving up and down, grunting, and lots of sweating (weird). Once it was over I didn't feel a thing, I was numb. I got up got dressed, went home, and ran me bath because he had cause some bleeding to occur.

    While taking my bath, I kept replaying my first day of summer and my first sexual experience with a high-school boy like the popular girls from my middle. It was just one problem for me, it was nothing like they described. I was not in love afterwards like they boasted and it was not one of those experiences I would cherish for the rest of my life. I felt nothing. Crap, was it something wrong with me? Did I do it wrong? Was I supposed to do something else to feel what they felt? I contemplated for hours while replaying the day's events in my mind and not realizing what irresponsible thing I had just did to myself. I did not understand what my pearls were at this age because all the girls were doing it.

My high-school boyfriend had become really attached to me and pressuring me to have sex again. I was totally uninterested in him or having sex again because there had been no emotional connection made from that experience just pain. He was furious and would follow me everywhere. He really became angry when my attention became occupied with another boy. That was the end of my first summer fling.

My unofficial sexual education from the more experienced girls that were in my middle school class never spoke of the pain that sex could invade your body. Even my first summer fling with my then high-school boyfriend would not prepare me for the evils that lurk. Sadly, no one told me sex could be used to cause a lifetime of pain physically and emotionally when placed in the hands of the wrong people.

As a teenager, I had become a reckless, numb, and non-stop party girl. I was a disconnected young woman, hiding my struggles in my rebellion, screaming for help with no one to listen. My relationships, or shall I say my "situationships" with boys mirrored my self-destruction.

Self-destruction can be mental, physical, financial, or emotional. I had experienced so much trauma that I had become cold, unemotional, and unable to properly develop a great foundation for a healthy relationship. The following experiences detailed below had a strong negative influence on my life.

To cope I had adapted to my circumstances, adjusted my state of mind, and how I would approach any interaction with a male counterpart going forward. I had begun to objectify men the same way they did women. I would be very elusive, never allowing them ever to venture to my home, kept any emotion of out the situation to the point they doubted if I ever liked them, and I never showed weakness to anyone not one ounce of vulnerability. I would never show any signs of emotion, listen to slow songs, or watch love stories to block out any emotion.

For years after these events, I would continue to meet men with a not so good background, but the fast money, the emotional detachment, and no commitment was just right for me at that reckless time in my life. I had drowned out the pain, suppressed the trauma, partied, and drank my way through it all. I was running from myself hard and running nowhere truly, because I still had to live with me one way or another. I was lost, suffered from trauma, grief, and emotional disconnect on all levels. I had not yet reached the moment that I had understood that my suppression of all my trauma was spiraling my life out of control. Yet because I had convinced myself that I was having the time of my life and I was on top of my game while looking like I had it all together I continued. I will go onto to explain that more in the chapter "The Birth of the Overachiever."

Bo, was a sweet-talking, stalking, abusive playboy when we met, and I was just 17 or 18 years old. He had moved from another state and was now residing here in Baltimore with his brother. He was the sweetest person I had met in a long time and wowed even my parents on some occasions with gifts for all of us. Although I didn't know it at the time he had a sketchy past. I used to think his desire to spend a lot of time with me was the cutest thing going… until it became obsessive.

We would go on elaborate dates, hang out, travel, and have a good time with one another. He gave me whatever I wanted and money was never a problem. But, it would eventually all come with high a cost. Bo, never let me go out with my friends or spend time with my family alone; he also demanded to come along on every outting. It was becoming impossible to spend time with my family or even myself. The more I tried to regain my independence or space from him the crazier he got.

I found myself in a crazy situation that only got crazier by the minute. I would look up from my desk at work, and he would be standing there, staring at me, only to begin 21 questions.

I became depressed, withdrawn from my friends, scared, and unable to gain control of my life at this point. I'm a true Aquarian and answering questions or losing my freedom was not sitting well with me. He had become very controlling and begin to stalk me every chance he got.

One weekend we decided to travel to all-star weekend in Philly to have a great time, party, and enjoy the excitement of being there – or so I thought...

The physical abuse had started because he noticed other men noticing me. As I felt pain come across my face I became dazed for a second and unaware of the advanced attention made by other men. He threw his first punch to the left side of my face while I sat in the passenger side of the car looking out of the window trying to block him out. I was so focused on enjoying the evening but his anger grew to uncontrollable. Then the second punch came and this time I could shield myself from the impact this time. Of course, I'm not the docile type. I threw a punch back with just as much force. We continued to fight for a couple of minutes while tussling back and forth until he got tired. I was relieved and in shock at the same time at what just happened. But, because I was in another state with no one to help me, embarrassed, and not wanting to bring attention to myself I said nothing. The girl that came along with us told me that her and her then boyfriend fought the same way. She also had the nerve to tell me it would be okay.

> Dumb girl: Girl me and my boyfriend fight like that all the time (as she begins to laugh) it will be ok.
>
> Me: Bitch please this is not acceptable
>
> Dumb girl: He still loves you. Let's just continue to have fun
>
> Me: this is not love (side eye). Fuck your fun I am ready to go home (as I took a sip of my first of several drinks that night)

In my heart, I knew it would not be ok but I had no idea what to do. My only initial solution was to numb my pain by getting so drunk I eventually blacked out for the rest of the night barely remembering where else we went.

I woke up praying to the porcelain god, puking my life up, and had no idea how we made it to a hotel room in Philly. He was like Dr. Jekel and Mr, Hyde he was acting as if nothing happened the night before. Bo was being super nice, attentive, and wanting to take care of me while I was sick with a major hangover. We got up went to breakfast in silence because I was still on edge from the previous night and he was just to calm to trust.

Once we got home I tried to leave Bo on several occasions, but the stalking got worse, and so did his threats. The physical abuse, fights, and arguments continued with intensity. He would turn on me at the drop of dime. I found myself feeling like I had to continuously walk around on eggshells around him not to anger him or send him into a rage. It had gotten so bad that we would be out in public, he could no longer control his anger, and the fighting was no longer behind closed doors. Emotionally drained, depleted, and embarrassed I would just try to quickly walk away when I felt him getting started.

I turned down his sexual advances one night after we had trying evening at dinner and I was not in the mood for intimacy. Bo was not happy at all and begin to accuse me of dealing with other men. He accusations were something I was use to because a man could simply look my way and he would insist what I was flirting with the man. But, this time was completely different from any other time. I was bracing myself for the fight that was coming only this time it didn't come.

Bo forced me into the other room not uttering a word with a glazed look on his eyes. As he forced me into the other room he was ripping my clothing off damn near destroying them as he did so. This rage I seen in him was not like the other typical time we had fought and new devil had reared his ugly head. He grabbed me by my hair, turned me around, and bent me over forcing his penis in me with all the strength he could muster up damn near flipping us on to the floor. He wrapped one hand around my throat and told me bitch you will never leave me or deny me what belongs to me ever in your life. As he began to rape me in my own house, like it was a game, and laughing along the way I would black out at times to hide the pain. In between the threats, the forceful thrust, and his chocking until he could hear not breath coming from my body I went completely numb. Limp almost praying he would stop but he just kept going. He finally got tired and fell asleep on top of me. Unable to move, cry, or express any emotion I waited for him to roll over so I could make it to the bathroom. I sat in the shower for what seemed like hours trying to make any noise to wake him. I also questioned

God and why would he allow someone to treat me like this. But the real why not why God but Why would I allow it? Truth is I was afraid of Bo and what I knew he was capable of.

I felt so violated, angry, helpless, and disappointed in myself for allowing this vile piece of a man do these things to me. Again, I felt like I had no one to go to, I was embarrassed, and I didn't want to involve anyone into my drama. I had already experienced and knew how crazy Bo was. I wanted to keep the peace within my family because we had already got through so much with the death of my brother a couple years prior so I blocked it out. It would be months before I could get away from Bo.

I guess God heard my inner cries or recognized my inability to walk away because Bo was arrested and placed in jail on drug charges for a couple of years. But, my recovery from the trauma and abuse that Bo had inflicted would not come for several years down the road. I suppressed the events for survival or was it because I was embarrassed. Girl, I must be honest I was embarrassed. But, what suppression never taught me was how to protect myself because it would happen again.

One night introduced me to the self-imposed rule that I would never let a date come pick me up leaving me at the mercy of anyone else going forward. For years, I would only meet men at our destination for our date, never disclosing where I lived, or giving control being held captive ever again.

It was Friday night and I had agreed to go on a date with a Tim, who I met at the club a couple weeks prior. We agreed to dinner and drinks having a fantastic time. After dinner, we sat in the car and talked for a while. Tim finally decided to pull off still talking about how much a great time we had over dinner and laughing about or previous conversations. As we were driving, laughing, and talking while staring out of the window the route we were taking to my house had begun to look unfamiliar.

>Where are, we going? This does not look like the way to my house? I asked Tim

>Oh, I just need to stop pass my house for a second. Tim said.

>I must get up early for work Tim. This will not take, long will it? I explained.

>No, it will not take long we are almost there. Tim politely said.

Instead of my Tim taking me back to my home, he took me to his so-called house. As he parked the car he turned over to me and said it is too late to leave such a beautiful young lady in the car alone please come in and I will only be a minute. I shrugged my shoulders and repeated with irritation, ok only a minute. Once inside of his home, he ventured into another room. I waited with my coat sitting on the coach to go home for what felt like more than just a few minutes as Tim had promised. He would finally reappear back in to the Livingroom with a slight smirk on his face asking was I ok and why did I still have my coat on. In his mind, he had already made other plans. My response so you can take my ass home that why, I told you had to work in the morning. But, in the back of my mind I realized he had no intentions of doing so. At least, not at that moment was I going home. I was stuck, my car was home and I didn't have a phone.

Tim asked if we could chill for a while and then he would take me home in a stern voice while removing my coat. Not to anger him, I said sure and then explained again the importance of needing to get up very early for work. He shook his head okay as he came closer towards me for a kiss. I hated kissing, the thought of swapping spit with a complete stranger really freaked me out even more. I slowly turned my head away, stating that I don't like to kiss, but he forced me to do so. Oh shit, I thought to myself as his demeanor changed. It had happened again.

How could you be so stupid, I screamed at myself.

How are you going to get out of this one?

Just be nice and ask to go home again, ok!

Tim, I really don't think this is a good idea. Let's just call it a night and we will talk in the morning. As I explained.

(silence and stares) It's just a kiss calm the fuck down as he forced me back on the couch by my arm, Tim stated.

(talking to myself) SHIT that didn't work. (as I sat in silence)

I was caught in a situation in a similar situation like with Bo but with a stranger. The only thing I had learned from my situation with Bo was to block out the events and try not to make him angry. That didn't teach me a damn thing what the hell was I supposed to do now in this situation. As I sat there with this strange guy who I thought was so nice shoving his nasty tongue down my throat I went dumb. He became focused, more aggressive, and determined to get my clothes off. I guess he was in the moment but I had drifted off into the land of oh shit and what fuck did I get myself into. For survival, I had only adapted to numbing myself, doing little to anger the person, and excepting my defeat praying it would be all over before I knew it.

He slowly removed my clothes as his digesting spit swapping persisted. With slight resistance, his force became stronger but he never spoke a word. The only thing I could say to myself is, please let me get through this night as fast as possible. I asked God, why did I deserve this happening to me again? What did I do so wrong to be faced with so much harm? To not further anger Tim, I stayed quiet, numb, and afraid to speak I let him violate my body. Again, fear had one and so did Tim that night. As I laid there stiff as a board Tim trusting his manhood in between my legs I vowed to never date again. It was finally over still scared to move I waited for him to offer me a means to clean myself up pretending that he performance was good. Once I was fully dressed unable to shed a tear, or show any emotion with a soft voice I asked him to take me home he obliged this time.

The drive home felt long as faked as if I was sleeping just so I would not have to engage in conversation I felt my soul harden. I was angry mostly at myself because I felt weak. But, I was really to blame? I told myself I was? I bared the burden yet again, suppressed the pain, and normalized it to cope. I must have sat is the tub the remainder of the night until it was time for me to get dressed for work. I turned cold, my feelings of love, or dating had been forever changed. I'm shit, at that point I didn't believe it existed because surely, I wasn't capable of receiving love. I think God was punishing me for something!

After that night, I had to change the phone number and each time I saw him out in public, I tried to avoid him. This worked until the day he made a big ass scene in a large group of people. Tim had begun to accuse me of being his cheating girlfriend and asking me why did I leave him. I felt so low, embarrassed, but also angry mostly at myself. I was in a paralyzed state, trying to act like he was not talking to me, and continued to talk to a friend as if I could not hear the commotion taking place right before my eyes. I quickly walked away without shedding one tear my emotional attachment to situations had died. After that day, I never say him again for many years and even when we made eye contact as sense of fear tingled throughout my body as I turned to walk in the opposite direction.

Some of us try to justify the actions of others, we look for love even in the most unloving situation, or place blame on ourselves as the root cause of such traumatic events, even when this is untrue. We may want each encounter or relationship to be healthy and happy but sometimes it does not pan out that way you hope. The relationship may begin well, only to come to that forlorn conclusion that the relationship just isn't working out. Usually, this conclusion does not happen in an instant.

There are various types of abuse; physical, emotional, verbal, and sexual. We all have a clear understanding of what physical abuse is. But it is important to understand that even if there are no marks left behind, abuse is abuse. When it comes to emotional and verbal abuse, we are referring to abusive language as well as degrading comments. Any time sex is used as a tool or weapon it is wrong.

Abusive partners find ways to twist the circumstances so that the blame is always yours. Besides using humiliation as a weapon, he or she attempts to control your life in ways that a partner should not. He or she may demand that you dress a certain way or refrain from doing something that seems harmless. He or she may threaten you or threaten to harm themselves if things do not go their way.

Abusive relationships are never healthy. A healthy relationship is built upon the foundations of respect, consideration, and trust. If you are involved in a relationship which lack these foundations, then it is time to make some immediate changes. I always say that you cannot give love appropriately if you do not love and care for yourself first. It is time to put yourself first. Take the initial steps toward the future that you deserve and get help now!

> **Victimization is defined as causing someone to be treated unfairly or made to feel as if he/she is in a bad position (dictionary.com).**
>
> **Rape is defined as unlawful sexual activity usually involving sexual intercourse carried out forcibly or under threat of injury. (Merriam-Webster.com)**

Now, don't jump to any crazy conclusions, I have had the opportunity to have some amazing relationships. Because I was unaware of the damage those previous bad relationships had truly caused me I was unable to properly love those who needed me to love them back in a healthy way. I was detached, cold in some cases, and uncommitted which was very unhealthy, especially for a woman.

One thing that I didn't know then that I understand now is each relationship is composed of two unique individuals. Both of you have your separate histories, your influences, your wants and needs, your hopes, dreams, emotions, and perspectives. This is great because if you were both the same you would have a very boring relationship. We need the differences in relationships to spark new thoughts and ideas and to drive the relationship forward. Our differences can make life interesting, but there are times when our differences are just too pronounced. Overcoming relationship differences is a real test of diplomacy and one which will decide if your relationship will survive.

When you ask yourself about past or current relationships, here are some things to reflect on:

- **What kind of expectations did you have?**
- **Were they realistic or unrealistic?**
- **Who did your partner fall in love with, was it you or was it someone that you are not?**

Our views on relationships are shaped from when we are children, and we start with our parents' relationship, and as we grow older. We receive fresh input from novels, television, Hollywood and our personal experiences.

It wasn't until I completely and unapologetically self-assessed that I could identify my previous trauma was the problem, which I had suppressed. The trauma was one of the root causes for my unhealthy foundation which I unknowingly brought to each of my relationships.

With the help of feedback from past relationships gone wrong because of the trauma I experienced I received a unique perspective of my behaviors, which gave me the ability to fully analyze my pain on a larger scale. It was also painfully obvious that women were meant to love and exude love, which was something I was unequipped to do. I was emotionless. I knew I had some major work to do, so I did what I do best I started to educate myself on trauma and abuse side effects, adverse behaviors, and undeveloped emotional foundations. I went to counseling for a couple years while working personally and spiritually to develop a healthy relationship with myself first.

Some of the steps I had taken during this time included getting to know myself first, date me, and truly learn what love meant to me to properly assist others on how to love me as well. As I did the work, to get over the trauma from abuse. The amount of work I had put in would be nearly destroyed, depleted, and shredded beyond recognition which will be explained in the upcoming chapter The Betrayal.

An open letter to myself:

Have you ever wondered if you would be enough? Let's face it, you are damaged goods, right? Besides, didn't everyone see me as trash, impure, used and abused on so many levels as I did? Just rotten, unlovable trash, right? **No! Wrong!** You are a Beautiful, extremely loved, loveable queen in her purest form of God's grace.

But, how could you be loved, let alone love properly, surely everyone could your brokenness, right? They had every right to treat you as if the pieces of you were never meant to be put back together, right? **Wrong!** Those who were unable to love themselves or may have not experienced a healthy dose of love tried to rob you of your ability to love appropriately. Love, is you, love is in you, and love deserves you.

Yes, even in all your flaws, visible or invisible to the naked eye, queen, God never left you even when man did. Even in the moments you felt alone, you were never truly alone, Beautiful.

In the moments when you feel the most exposed, fighting to hide your vulnerability, God knows that He is stripping you down to rebuild you back up new. Even if you have traveled among the depths of the worst valleys, Queen, God has never left you. He guided you along the way. With each step, you have taken He has walked beside you, molding you to learn the lessons he has placed before you that you can endure what life will bring to your feet.

God's lesson is for you to trust in Him, even when your trust has been broken by man. You were born to love, receive love, and live a life surround by love, no matter the situation. Own it, Queen!

YOU ARE LOVE! LET NO MAN TELL YOU OTHERWISE.

If you are anything like me, maybe you blamed yourself for the things that happened to you.

If so, list your reasons why below. Then, apologize to yourself, gorgeous. You are not to blame!

_____
_____
_____
_____
_____
_____
_____
_____

List the things hindering you from regaining your self-confidence.

_____
_____
_____
_____
_____
_____
_____
_____

Now let's dig deep and list as many reasons as you can to tell yourself how beautiful you are Chica:

_____
_____
_____
_____
_____
_____
_____
_____

Here are a few books/guides and YouTube channels I used to help me regain my confidence, restore my trust in myself, and push pass the pain honey (just to name a few):

- In the Meantime: Finding Yourself and the Love You Want (Inyanla Vanzant)
- The Alchemist (Paulo Coelho)
- The Value in The Valley: A Black Woman's Guide Through Life's Dilemmas (Inyanla Vanzant)
- Keys to Success: The 17 Principles of Personal Achievement (Napoleon Hill)
- Oprah (YouTube)
- Eric Thomas (YouTube)
- Sarah Jakes (YouTube)

BOUNCE BACK 2:

I Dated Death

Death was jealous and took so many people I loved. Death was cold, unforgiving, and unwilling to compromise based upon my feelings. Death always got what he wanted no matter the trail of hurt he left behind. I walked away a few times but he was like a thief in the night stalking everyone close to me waiting to make his move. I know you're thinking to yourself, well who is death, right? Death is the one thing none of us can avoid in our lifetimes, death is all around us, and death with his bitch ass even takes the ones we love before we are ready for them to leave us.

I was 14 years old when I started experiencing death around me at an alarming rate, with no outlet or education on how to properly grieve at a healthy level. With tears in my eyes, even years later, it feels like yesterday recanting how these moments dating death had rocked my world at a catastrophic level.

Each year was a new dance and a new fight to hold on to my soul not allowing Death to steal it had become exhausting. Why did I have to fight so hard? Why did death choose me, of all people, to date? Was he after me too? Or, was he after my mind?

My first real introduction to death and his violence had begun. The year was 1996, Resonable Doubt (JayZ), Hard Core (Lil Kim), All Eyez on Me (TuPac), ILL NaNa (Foxy Brown), and Ice Cream Man (Master P) to name a few were setting the streets on fire and it was the best musical year to date in my opinion. I was just entering in the ninth grade and you couldn't tell me anything, I was in high-school. Unfortunately, it was the also the year the death decided he wanted to form an ongoing relationship without my consent.

We all had those crazy cool older male cousins that we looked up to, you know. Mines was smart, fun to be around, and had the best fiancé I had ever met. Not to mention she was also my fun neighbor, what a coincidence. Donte, was in college to become a special education teacher, expecting his first baby, and preparing to get married soon. Boy, was he something to admire you know. Girls dream of building relationships with guys who had their shit together.

1996, my cousin set out to celebrate his birthday with a night full of fun and adventure. But, instead my aunt was receiving a phone call to come an identify her child body. That year my older cousin was murdered the day before his birthday outside of Volcano's Night Club and I remember it like it was yesterday. When you are exposed to the violent death of a loved one and it is not from natural causes something inside of you dies along with them. The only thing I could replay in my mind was, all he wanted to do was celebrate his birthday, not his death day. My heart was broken and the coldness had begun to slowly invade my heart.

I can remember our family all gathering at my aunt's house for details and to comfort one another. I was sitting on the steps with my uncle, fixated on a damn Rubix cube, just turning it repeatedly and unable to connect with my emotions. I was fully enraged with anger. I was so into trying to transfer my anger to that Rubix cube thingy that my uncle snatched it from me, probably hoping I would cry, yell, or do something to release the emotions I was feeling. It was at that moment it became completely apparent that I was unable to connect with my emotional state or able to grieve. As I look back on that moment, I wonder, was I afraid to show emotion? Or was I in shock?

How do you define grief? And are you able to grieve in a healthy manner?

_____
_____
_____
_____
_____
_____
_____

Unfortunately, for me along the way I started to lose multiple friends and some family members on a yearly basis I did not grieve in a healthy manner. As the family faced a long process with the funeral, coming to terms with never seeing my cousin again, and the criminal trial that awaited turned into a reoccurring nightmare repeatedly. I was young unable to grasp how this moment, and others, like it would forever change my life.

_____

In 1998, news of my friend and classmate broke. Tee, had been murdered while walking to the store with a friend. Was this a sick joke that the universe was playing on me? No, but a harsh reality with a face full of tears and a mouth full of questions, like how could someone be so callous? We had just met up on the number 15-bus stop in the morning the week prior trying to make our way to school together not before stopping at Lexington market to grab food for lunch. Our cafeteria food was horrible and sometime we would leave school and venture out to the local carry out to get chicken boxes together.

Should a beautiful bright young woman with a heart of gold go on to be with the Lord, before she had the chance to reach her full potential? I could honestly say I was not pleased with God for allowing death to take my friend away from in such a horrific way. Aren't people supposed to die of old age and illness with names we are unable to pronounce? Why in the hell were the people around me being taken so young? I'm sure once the news was shared, it took the breath out of every friend, classmate, and staff member at my high school that year.

What I struggled with most was she was not only a friend, she was my age, and it made it all too real that your mortality can be challenged at any age not just from those life sucking diseases that we can't pronounce.

Reality check upon reality check followed. More news continued to break about others being murdered during my years in high school on a regular basis. I attempted to regain my composure, but it was hard. With the growing coldness in my heart, the connection to others had started declining as well as my ability to fully focus in school. The growing trend of clothing became RIP memorabilia. It shouldn't be a trend for anyone, especially young people, but it was for us.

In July 1999, my heart completely froze. I became very disconnected from my emotions or any ability to get close to another human being that required any type of emotional connection after my brother died. My brother and I were four years apart in age and before hormones took over we were partners in crime together. I was the true definition of a tomboy and the annoying little sister who like to follow he brother around doing whatever he wanted to do. On some occasions the actives that we engaged in like jumping off the garage roof in the back of our apartment on to pissy mattresses probably could have killed us or broken our necks. (laughs) Thank goodness, we never cause any major injuries to our bodies on that day. Or, when Christmas rolled around and we would go hunting for our gifts and play with them while my mom was at work. Priceless moments. Unfortunately, I have no recollection of the details of my last interaction with him, only to be told it was an argument of sorts. Also, there are very few things I remember from the day of my brother's funeral or even some of our childhood memories. It's like my brain erased some of the major parts of my life. At least I have pictures to reminisce with you know.

My brother died the day before my nephew's third birthday, leaving behind his only son. I remember clearly hearing a phone call come into to a family friend's cell phone asking for them to bring me home immediately. The mood and tone had immediately changed with an eerie silence that filled the car. I was not told the reason why our evening activities had been cut short, only that we needed to get to my parents' house right away.

As we pulled up, many people had already gathered in my house. which was very odd, because let's face it, that only happens on holidays or funerals. What I was about to hear coming through my ears no one could have ever prepared me for - I mean *no one*.

After hearing the news of my brother's death, I just remember running out of my house, just to breathe because so many fake ass unknown people had gathered at my house, like a circus. Like, why? Why do people do that to families, with no intentions on truly being there when it's needed the most, post-funeral? Why? I snapped, completely shutting down, and shutting everyone out.

I briefly saw the detectives standing in the living room of my house as I went from the staircase, straight out of the front door gazing at the vultures who were sitting around like gossip columnists waiting to hear the findings while passing by the pit of hell, as I called it. Day in and day out, I would leave out of the house in the morning to avoid the spectacle and come in late night, praying they would be gone.

I was completely numb, lost, and angry. I went into a very deep dark place, barely eating, sleeping, or socializing. I did everything to prepare for my brother's funeral alone which kept my mind clear and me out of trouble. I would take the truck and during my long drives, sometimes to nowhere, I would zone out to the last CD my brother listened before he died - Jay-Z classic, "Reasonable Doubt". That CD become my therapy, my anthem, and my blueprint for learning how to bounce back. To this very day, that CD gives me a calm that I could never explain. It's like my brother and I are cruising, just zoning, trying to figure out this thing we call life alone.

On the day of the viewing I did not shed one tear. I don't even remember going in to the funeral home to view his body. The day of his funeral I blacked out. Child, I could not tell you who, what, where, or how many people were there. Nothing about that day seemed real. It became a fog of a memory I try to tap into, but I can't find the secret code for entry. It's like my brain locked it away; never for me to bear witness to what that day held for me. Maybe it's only right that I am not privy to the details for my own protection. Who knows. On that day, my mom's heart had broken in too many pieces, and I had to be strong for the three of us, including my nephew.

Post the aftermath of the funeral a new Ebony was born cold, disconnected, emotionally detached, non-affectionate, and unwilling to get close or stay close to anyone individual for too long. As time progressed I had attended countless funerals, until my high school love was murdered some years later. His funeral was the last funeral I attended, if it was not my immediate family member, for a long time. I had acquired more obituaries of young people losing their lives it became the norm.

With countless questions that continue to go unanswered the main one I still ask today is: How could a civilian child or any adult recover from PTSD or grieve on a healthy level when they are living amongst a war zone daily on U.S. soil? My healing would not come for some years later but my questions are still up for debate.

> **PTSD is defined as a mental health condition that is triggered by a terrifying event or experience witnessed. Symptoms may include flashbacks, nightmares, severe anxiety, as well as uncontrolled thoughts about the events. All of these symptoms I have experienced at one moment or another.**
> **(Mayoclinc.com)**

Grief

__How to Go On Living When Someone You Love Dies, By: Therese A. Rando, PhD.__, has helped me to acknowledge takeaway points about grief. My understanding from what I learned in 1999 is vastly different now in 2016. I encourage anyone struggling with grief to invest in this book or similar text for a better understanding and an approach on how to cope with grief. I also encourage you to find a great grief counselor. It wasn't until years later that I invested into counseling for a about two years and it was a blessing when I found the right one. Honey, let me tell you I went through a couple counselors before I found the right special person as I affectionately called her.

> **Grief is defined as keen mental suffering or distress over affliction or loss; sharp sorrow; painful regret.**
>
> **(dictionary.com)**

According, to Grief.com there are 5 stages of grief:

- Denial
- Anger
- Bargaining
- Depression
- Acceptance

These 5 stages are the natural flow of how an individual is supposed to grieve in a healthy manner. But, there are many instances where this is not the case and the natural processed is disrupted or non-existent.

Grieving can have a major strong hold especially when you are constantly experiencing loss after loss. The steps in the grieving process are meant to bring you back to a healthy relationship with yourself and the separation from your loved one. It's the inability to grieve on a healthy level once everyone goes home after the funeral and you are left alone to cope with your loss.

How have you coped with grief in your own life?

_____

How do you define grief? What does grief look like, feel like, and sound like to you?

_____

Have you properly found the time and help to grieve in a healthy manner? If not create a plan below to get healthy today. You owe it to yourself!

_____
_____
_____
_____
_____
_____
_____
_____

Bounce Back 3:

The Birth of The Over Achiever

I was a young, inquisitive child who loved to excel in every way possible. Shout out to my mom who would punish us by making us do book reports on a regular basis and made frequent library trips mandatory. I have struggled so much throughout my journey with being okay to display my excitement to learn and to embrace being smart in certain areas. It's funny today as I embrace being a pretty nerd who loves books more than anything I was ashamed. I rarely watch television; I enjoy YouTube for educational purposes, and I am constantly looking for material to help me grow in every area of my life. Super nerdy huh?

Once I entered high school, I had forgotten most of what I had learned in middle school due to extracurricular activities. Activities were worshiped at my high school, so I joined many clubs and became class officer. After the loss of my brother right before my senior year of high school, my interest in school declined. I begin to engage in self-destructive activities and started partying a lot to numb the pain. When it came time to apply for colleges my grades had deteriorated, not so low that I was in fear of failing, but not good enough to get into an IVY league college. I had no intentions on going away to college but I still felt like it was an option for me no matter what. My SAT scores were low and I was not prepared enough to take such a massive exam to measure work that I honestly did not do while in high school. Unfortunately, testing was not something I enjoyed either, it gave me great anxiety. When it came time for me my SATs I did what anyone who was not prepared to take a measurement test would do. Shit, I stared out the window for most of the test, very uninterested. I knew the weight the test held for me to get into certain colleges but unable to concentrate or focus everything on the test looked foreign to me.

The plan to start looking for colleges during my senior year of high school was extremely stressful because I had experienced so much trauma up to this point and my focus was way off. I tried to talk with my high school guidance counselor in the process of applying for college but the only thing she told me was that I was not college material and I should use my trade (business) as my career. Long-story short what she was basically telling me was that I should settle and give up my dreams of one day attaining my college degree. Once that statement was made to me, the only thing it did was ignite a fire of pure determination in me that has been lit ever since. Even though I had mentors, administrators, and teachers that had my best interest in mind, while trying to keep me on the right track, the pain of my brother recent death was stronger. I was fortunate to have those influences that allowed me to work in the main office during my last years in high school and for two years after I graduated until I figured it out.

I never told my parents or anyone about that statement made to me until later in life, but that was one more disappointment that has helped to birth the overachiever you see before today. Or, as I would affectionately call it the pretty nerd honey. But, because I never attended college tours or had any guidance in the process, I enrolled myself into the local community college without a plan. With determination, I knew I needed to start from somewhere.

After a year or two at community college, I transferred myself to a four-year university where I faced adversity again with a blatant racist teacher where my grades suffered. But, giving up was never in the cards even though I was failing horribly.

I found my way to another university where I later graduated from with my baccalaureate degree double majoring in sociology and anthropology. It was after I met this amazing secretary who assisted me selecting a double major that my vision became clear and attainable. I worked and went to school seven days a week to finish my bachelor's degree. Boy, was it the most exhausting experience ever. I would be on the phone with my mother in tears suffering from exhaustion. It didn't help that I was addicted to Starbucks and Mountain Dew at the time, talk about an emotional over caffeinated disaster. It was a pivotal moment for me to prove to my old high school guidance counselor that I was college material, as well to myself, that you are more than the labels that people try to put on you. I did face some adversity at that school, but it was more motivation to prove that I did belong there.

I discovered that it was not only about what's going on in your life right now, but it is also about what you want for yourself. We are all different from each other, and we have different types of orientations. Breaking through discouragement can make some people focus on what they want to achieve, while others may be badly affected by the discouragement.

Are you faced with a tough situation, something that should have been easy, but for some reason it just isn't turning out that way you intended it to? We have all been there, and everyone knows what that situation is like. No one likes it. However, that situation is not solved by giving up and walking away. You can persevere and get through to the other side by never giving up.

Life doesn't have to be difficult, but it does often end up being just that. Often, we are faced with decisions we would rather not make, working for someone we would rather not, doing something we would rather not do all for less money than we would rather make. Many people dream of breaking out of that situation; we dream of being able to do what we love and being able to make a living at it. How exactly does that happen? How do you make those dreams come true? You boldly must challenge yourself! Make sure that you are throwing all the negative forces around you away and that you are proving all the negative people wrong. That alone should encourage you to do more. Think of how they belittle you and decide in your heart to surprise them. I continue to have a 'conquer and defeat' attitude with everything I seek to accomplish.

I would go on to graduate again from a community college with an AA degree in respiratory therapy and again two years later with a certification in sleep therapy. I am currently an adjunct professor at that community college I graduated from in the Sleep Therapy Program, the CEO of Ambitionz R Us LLC, and author of *'The Art of Bouncing Back: How I survived it all'*.

Never allow anyone to write or rewrite your dreams for you, destroy your ambition, or belittle your aspirations. You were meant to walk in your greatness, no matter your past mistakes, struggles, trials, or tribulations.

Take pride and embrace your inner overachiever! Never let the negativity of others hinder you from pursuing your ambitions.

Have you been labeled as an overachiever? If so, has it affected you negatively? Why?

_____
_____
_____
_____
_____
_____

How are you mastering your goals lists? Do you make one?

If not, create your first one below:

_____
_____
_____
_____
_____
_____
_____
_____
_____
_____

What steps are you taking to stay completely focused and block out distractions?

If none, create some below:

_____
_____
_____
_____
_____
_____

It's time to own your crown, embrace your nerdy side, and dominate in your lane, queen. Say it loud and proud: I am overachiever and I own that ish like a boss!

Bounce Back 4:

A Father's Betrayal

The betrayal had been brewing for years but the lid was about to blow off before we all realized it. It was February 15, 2014 a week after my birthday my life would change forever on that night. I was not feeling well this day, I had papers due for my master's courses, and the snow had been ridiculous a couple days previously. I had been on the phone with my parents because my mother had surgery a couple weeks prior and I was worried about my father shoveling snow so I had been trying to find him a snow blower online.

Hey mom, how are you feeling? Do you need anything?

I'm ok just having some pain but I am fine, as my mom replies.

Hey you didn't ask how I was doing? as my father yells in the phone.

I was online looking for a snow blower for you. I'm afraid with all the snow fall and shoveling can be a bit much for your heart.

As my father clears his throat, Ok sounds good. (silence) So, kid what are you doing tonight?

I'm not sure yet. Why?

Oh, nothing I must leave out to go to work for a few so check on your mother, Good bye Kid.

Ok!

I was set to attend a charity dinner that night with my cousin but because I was not feeling well I was not sure if I was attending. I decided to get dress, sick and all, to attend this event with my cousins. It was a nice event, with great food and drink. I was on my way to the restroom with my cousin when my heart dropped as I thought I seen a replica of my father. It was him, so, as I told my cousin, 'Wait, let me back up to see if that's who I think it is.' My heart was beginning to beat very fast as I begin to look.

As I stood there in disbelief still questioning myself, is this really happening to me? I stared at my father, who was attending the same party I was with another woman who looked around my age. I collapsed inside at that moment not knowing how to react but with an awkward yet scary calm that glazed over me. As I proceeded to ask him what he was doing there and who was this woman he begin to act as if he didn't know me which further escalated the issue.

Who are you? As I stand there in disbelief.

Oh, I am his fiancé (flashes her ring), says the slut

He is a married man, sweetheart, as I roll my eyes.

She didn't say that (with a look of disbelief on his face), my father responds sarcastically.

As she stared at me like I was another one of his women I kindly told her that I was his daughter and again stated that he is married man of more than 30 years.

My father just sat there looking down, as I asked how could you do that? Mom was home alone post-surgery while you're out whoring around. He refused to answer me, but the young woman was very eager to answer all my questions. As his secret life began to be exposed he quickly requested to speak with me in the hallway. As we are exiting the main ballroom, he had begun to threaten me if I told my mother he would move out and leave her destitute. First, I couldn't believe my ears but now I couldn't believe my ears. As, the man I knew as my father had dissolved every ounce of decency he had left to threaten his only child whom he knows does not play. Because, I had already been through so much trauma the anger inside of me had been waiting to blow.

My reply was legendary. 'God blessed me with the ability to care for the both of us with my new career and I make more than enough money so you can do so.' I proceeded to call my mother as my father and I walked into the hallway. Because my relationship with my father had always been strained over the years and my respect level with him was minimal, I never feared him, so his approach never shook me. As we begin to argue in the hallway, he formulated lies even after the young woman gave me responses to all my questions. He would even go as far to say that he was not there with her, but they were the only two people at that table. So, as he kept lying, I became angrier at the lack of responsibility he was taking for tonight's events. I had enough of his ridiculous lies and I went to get the young lady so she could kindly bring some clarity to the situation as he followed behind me. Once we were all in each other vicinity the moment escalated. My father took his hand a mushed me by my head to keep me from getting to the young lady as they walked off hand and hand.

At that very moment, my father was no longer my father but another man that had betrayed his family and more importantly his flesh and blood with no remorse. My heart had instantly hardened yet again but this time it was not cold, it turned into the toughest army grade steel you could find (yup, that hard.).

There was no time to fall apart. I had to leave the party because we had already caused a major scene at a charity event that night. I tried my best to keep it together unable to shed a single tear, I felt sick, numb, angry, hurt, embarrassed, and disappointed. It was the same numbness I felt whenever I would experience a traumatic event. But, this time was different, I didn't retreat or block it out, I fought back.

I made my way home, changed my clothes and drove directly to my parents' house. Only things I can remember thinking to myself was, I must get to my mother; I need to get to my mother. Once I arrived to my parents' house, I was met by an aunt who I thank God was there to be with my mother until I got there.

I had to go into action, not only protect my mother, but myself as well. Any man willing to turn on his own child for a piece of ass in the street, you are not aware of lengths he will take in order to preserve is double life. The damage had been done, the locks were changed, phones were turned off, and I had to be there for my mother. By the morning, he started calling with threats, no remorse, and more lies just like the narcissist that he was.

> **A narcissistic personality is a mental disorder in which people have an inflated sense of their own importance, a deep need for admiration, and a lack of empathy for others. But behind the mask of ultra-confidence lies a fragile self-esteem that's vulnerable to the slightest criticism.**
>
> **(MayoClinic.com)**

Later that afternoon I had to go to my house to pick up my medication and a quick change of clothes because no one knew what was going to come next. As I pulled up to my house I could see my father and my aunts husband standing in my door way. As I looked closer you could see them changing the locks on my doors where I grew up, paid the mortgage, and had been doing so for over 11 years. The caveat of this situation was my house was in my father's name because it was my parents first house so he felt like he could give and take as he pleased. I exit my car slowly assessing the situation and to also maintain my composure because I could believe how my life was unfolding at this point. But, child it would go from bad to worst. I looked both men fully in their eyes and walked right passed them shaking my head as I entered the house. For a moment, I stopped and laughed as I looked back at two cowards changing the locks to my house because my father was caught being an adulterer. I had to laugh to keep from showing any emotion or letting the situation get the best of me. I guess my laughing pissed him off because he proceeded to say:

> You will not be able to keep your stuff in my house after you changed the locks on my doors at my house, as my father continued working not showing any emotion.

> I pay the mortgage here and all the bills here. So, you are just going to put me out of my house because you got caught fucking around on my mother? As I laugh while shaking my head.

> You don't have to worry about paying anymore bills and matter of fact make sure you get your stuff out of my house, my father yells.

> Rolls eyes and proceeds to call the police trying not cry.

After calling the police they told me it was nothing I could do because the house was in his name even though my belongings were physically there. The police tried to act as a mediator asking us both how did this domestic dispute come to this. The only thing the police could do was shake their heads at him and reply so you would do this to your own daughter? In full blown temper tantrum style, he replied yup, uhh huh with his hands folded, tapping his feet, and lips curled like a little boy. As he proceeded to tell me again while the police were present that I was not welcomed in either of his houses, finished changing the locks on my doors, and he was not giving me the keys I would have to leave the doors unlocked with all my possessions in the house until I got my stuff out.

My father is a snarky tone asked the police could he go and with disdain they replied yes. I would go into a long conversation with the officer's present about the moments leading up to the current situation they responded to. The officers tried their best to console me and help me as much as they could until my phone rang with my mother screaming on the other end of the phone.

My father in true fuck boy status had left my house and called the police on my sick mother because she told him he had to leave the house. So, I had to drop what I was doing at my house trying to safe guard my belongings to get to my mother. My father was causing havoc everywhere he went that day. As soon as I got to the house I picked up my mother who was distraught and angry as my father was taunting her once the police arrived. We went straight to the sheriff's office on that cold Sunday afternoon to obtain a temporary restraining order to keep him away from us. That night I knew we could not go back to our home so I took my mother to my grandmother's house.

The next day I had to scramble to call my friends as well as my cousins to help me pack my house up and move it all into storage before he came back to put my belongings out (or someone realized that the doors were not locked and stole them). We spent the day and most of the night backing up my whole life. All conversations were from a place of disbelief and denial amongst us all. I put all my possessions into storage locker not too far while frantically dealing with drama, as it came, for what seemed like an hourly basis.

It had been two days and things were getting worst by the day. Were exhausted, unable to eat because of the high amount of stress and trauma, and displaced from our home. Life as we knew it was no more and we had no idea what to do. It was time to find other living arrangements after realizing I was now homeless and unable to go to my parents' house because my mother was with me we went to a hotel for the night. With court the next day we had no idea what to expect.

That morning my mother went to the bank to get money for personal needs because at that time all we had was the clothes on our backs only to realize he had taking all the money out of the bank accounts and canceled them. As we tried to eat breakfast before court we had no idea how much worst the day would get. But shit got worse. Once we entered into the course house, my father was accompanied by his sisters, and brother in law who all with joy lied about us on the stand for him. As they taunted and belittled us on the stand in order to protect a person who had not only betrayed us but who would continue to hurt us in every way possible going forward. It was like in his twisted mind we were the ones caught doing wrong. Unfortunately, the judge did not grant our restraining orders that day we were devastated. Family had become just another word to me with no significant meaning unless their actions proved otherwise. Like Pac it was "me against the world" taking no shorts.

As we walked out of the courtroom I had two choices to make and I needed to make them fast. I could fall apart or I could go into grind mode to ensure that we would be well taken care of. Of course, I went into full grind mode. We continued to live in several hotels that I could get us great rates at, as I continued to work daily trying to keep it all together. I was also in my first semester of graduate school trying my best to complete my assignments on time with a clear mind. But, shit who was I kidding my brain was scrambled and anger invaded my body like a cancer. I was enrolled into two classes and I had been selected to sit on a board for my major, that I had to later turn down. Determined to maintain my courses I did the best I could to keep up finishing with one B and one C. So, my father started to continue to open up World War III, IV, V on me as he canceled my car insurance that I had paid up for 6 months, a month prior, cut my cell phone off that I had paid everyone's bill two weeks prior, and threatened to get me locked up on multiple occasions. He also had his sisters send threatening text messages on multiple occasions as if we did something wrong.

Each day, each situation, and each moment that was forced upon us let me know that loyalty was situational. My father's side of the family had turned their backs on us to protect a man in pursuits of destroying his own family. Can you believe that the people you do the most for are the quickest to betray you? Now, isn't that some shit for you to think about. Don't side eye me, yes, I know it's not everyone, but honey it has been a few questionable folks to go around. To continue with the betrayal while I worked, I gave my cousin money to take my mom out to eat and get her out of the hotel room. Chile, not knowing it would cost me my most expensive possessions that were housed in the trunk of my car because remember I was homeless at this point. I didn't realize from the distractions of the daily drama filled events going on that my belonging was missing until I went head out a realized that my designer bags, money, and other belonging were stolen by the very person I trusted to keep them safe. Because I had so many other things going on I had to move on from that moment while suffering more betrayal and heartbreak. I prayed to God for her in that moment and myself because I could not trust anyone at this point.

> **Trust is defined as firm belief in the character, strength, or truth of someone or something**
>
> **(Merriam-Webster.com).**

It would be almost a month and half before I found us somewhere to live and trying to keep it all together still residing in different hotels. Whatever my father could do to try to break us he tried it with malicious intent and no remorse all because he got caught living a double life unable to lie his way out of the results that would come. I would ask God often how could my own father throw me/his family away? What did I do to have suffered so much, but God would later reveal to my purpose within all of the pain I had endured.

I found a nice place for us to live in, but the moving process was rough and difficult. It was the tail end of the winter, we were exhausted, and getting assistance to move without alerting anyone to where we were moving was proving to be draining. I would go on to work every day both day shift and night to provide for us without complaint. I took my mother on a cruise for Mother's Day to try to ease the pain that we were going through and to be honest I need to get away as well just to breathe for a minute. I also took her to Virginia Beach and we spent time with my aunt just to get away as much as we could. As we proceeded to heal and gain some normalcy back I cooked for Thanksgiving and had the family over which helped us head into our first holiday season displaced from our homes.

Later that year my mother would need a full knee replacement because she was not able to properly heal from her surgery earlier in the year with us needing to move abruptly. I took every precaution to ensure that no one could access my mother during her surgery. As I sat there alone I came to the determination that my mother would not be place in any rehabilitation facility and that I would care for her at home.

Post recovery I stayed home with no pay to care for my mom post-surgery doing physical therapy at home twice a day, took her to physically therapy, and every appointment to ensure that she healed properly this time. She lovingly referred to me as Nurse Ratchet. We were very fortunate that year to spend Christmas and New Years at my cousin's house where we experienced so much love. Truthfully it was needed.

In that process, I also had the opportunity to enroll in the Sleep Program to increase my career portfolio, which would make things tight but I knew the opportunity was a must. My mother was recovering beautifully and eventually she would begin to work again. Emotionally we continued to work through everything as time progressed but we would still be met with some challenges. I would finish the sleep program months earlier than expected because I had to get back to working a full schedule in order to provide.

Fast forward to 2016. It had been almost two years before I had seen or heard from my father again until the moment I had to attend my grandmother's funeral early in the year. I had not seen her in over two years as well. I struggled and finally broke down once my grandmother passed because of my father I had not seen my grandmother because of his lies and erratic behavior we had been estranged. So, the only moment I had to see and spend time with my grandmother was looking at her in a casket. I shut the world off and stayed to myself with no communication with anyone for days. I could not understand why God was allowing me to go thru so much turmoil. A couple weeks later I would be turning 34 years old with a determination to get my life back on track. Because I had lost so much going through everything I fell into a deep depression. The events that led up to that moment had become overwhelming and I never had a moment to just cry or grieve. I stayed strong for all of us.

A turning point for me came for me after my birthday. My father's actions were not my fault. Our situation was not my fault, and his abandoning us was not my fault either. Silently I had carried the blame for all the fall out after that night, because our lives were turned upside down in every way possible. To me, the reason seemed to be that I decided to go out that one night, sick and all, on February 15, 2014. I would never ever forget.

> **Depression is defined as a state of feeling sad. A mood disorder marked especially by sadness, inactivity, difficulty with thinking and concentration.**
>
> **(Merriam-Webster.com)**

I would go on to get a great new job, win awards for great patient care, re-enroll back into my master's program, develop my business, do motivational speaking, and graduate from the sleep (Polysomnography) program. I became an adjunct faculty instructor at a community college, wrote this book, and reestablish a relationship with myself. Also, as part of my self-assessment journey as well as my healing I reached out to my father. Because of his resistance to acknowledge his role in the damage of our family, our relationship, and the effects of his actions has caused with unwillingness to apologize our relationship remains broken.

Our conversation did not bear any fruit towards growth, so at the end of our conversation he requested that I never call him again, something I must be okay with. This was not the first time he acted a complete ass - but this was the first time that his actions had completed destroyed our family, beyond the ability to rebuild. We all make mistakes in life, but when you set out to destroy the people who love you the most with malicious intent the character of a man is questioned, his reputation destroyed, and his karma with me and God decides. I try to remember the good days but can't help thinking about all that has been lost.

OPEN LETTER TO MY FATHER:

The first man a daughter falls in love with, if they have that opportunity, is her father. A father sets the tone for every man that will enter his daughter's life as the standard that she follows - the blueprint of relationships to come. A father shows her safety by keeping her safe from harm; how to value herself in the presences of boys; what respect is meant to feel like by how he treats her mother or the women in his life; and the value of her beauty in the midst of this ugly world.

A father is supposed to teach his children how to lead the pack not to follow the pack. A father is supposed to clothe, shelter, and feed his child or children. A father should be the epitome of its highest honor that has been bestowed upon him with the responsibility of life in his hands.

Even with tears in my eyes, as I defined what a father was supposed to look like to me my harsh reality has shown me that you sir, were further from what you were supposed to be to me. Even in your false glory of failed lies to how much you have contributed to my life you have done more damage than good. Yes, you have completed some good actions of forced kindness for recognition and to look good in the eyes of the masses. But, your truth will be told through my eyes to yours of how your narcissistic behaviors have ruined a family whose only aim was to love you and feel love back from you.

Growing up I watched you be unkind to my mother, my brother, myself, and others on several occasions in a sick a twisted game to you. Your job was to protect us but you continuously left us with nothing or in fear. Your job was to teach me how a man was supposed to love me but you were incapable. So, I had to learn through abuse, rape, and other traumatic events what love was not supposed to be to me. Your abandonment of you family has also proven of your inability to take responsibility for your actions.

You tried to destroy everything I worked for. You tried to break me, and you left me homeless. You tried to strip me of all my self-esteem, self-worth, and the ability to believe in love as you set in court and lied to our faces while trying to make us look bad with no remorse. I often wondered how a man could throw away not only his family but especially his own flesh and blood, but then I was quickly reminded that you are only repeating history. You were not properly loved as a child so now I could I expect you to be able to pass that down to me, right? How dare I expect my father to be the man he presented to the world to be that to his family, right?

As you have destroyed our relationship and what bond we did have sir you have taught me one of the best lessons in my life to date. You have taught me that loyalty is situational, love is fleeting from those who unable to fully love themselves, and I am not responsible for your inability to be a man. You have also taught me what a real man does not look like, how to completely stand on my own two feet, and how to provide for my family no matter what. You have also taught me that what I use to feel was not a lie that you were always disconnected from your family because you never knew who you were.

My prayer for you is that you get the healing that you need, you make peace with God for the lives you have destroyed, and that you realize a man is not based on the equipment that he has between his legs but on his ability to fully take care of his family lovingly without causing harm.

The saddest part about betrayal for me is that it has only come from family, former friends, and people I once loved the most. But the biggest gift that betrayal has given me is that GOD's light over me shines brighter than the darkness that others try to destroy me with and he has equipped me with the proper tools to Master the Art of Bouncing Back.

Like our last conversation before you told me never to call you again, I explained to you that I forgive you and I mean it. Yet, I just feel sorry for you not anger because you saw us as trash, while God has blessed us with loving people who see our value and the greatness we must offer the world.

God Bless

Love a heartbroken daughter

Have you been betrayed, abandoned, and/or hurt by your father? If so, how did it affect you?

_____
_____
_____
_____
_____
_____

Did the actions or non-actions of your father affect your relationships? If so, how are working to correct the disconnect?

_____
_____
_____
_____
_____
_____

Do you understand that you are not responsible for the insecurities or the irresponsibility's of your father?

If you do, get real and honest with yourself below listing the reason why you are not:

_____
_____
_____
_____
_____

Bounce Back 5:

The Healing

Healing is defined as the process of making or becoming sound or healthy again (Oxforddictionaraires.com). Healing is a very emotional, yet therapeutic process that each person must endure no matter the situation they are faced with (health, emotional, spiritual, or physical). The ideal of healing is very appealing but many shy away from the process or the valley they will be roaming through to get to the other side of what the healing process represents.

Healing and I mean truly healing, requires the most vulnerable version of yourself in all your flaws, scars, brokenness, and emotionally struggles to be revisited. I must be honest - I experienced every emotion that went along with this process - depression, fear, hurt, anguish - shit you name it, I went through it repeatedly until I pushed passed it. I had to get completely, unapologetically, coldhearted honest with myself to fully address everything.

My healing required me to fall in love with my own vulnerability. Vulnerability, is and has been a major challenge for me. To be vulnerable requires to give so much of yourself while traveling through the unknown. It exposes all of you to people who may or may not have your best interest at heart, it's like gambling which I don't enjoy. Until this point I was a part of the very resistant movement to vulnerability (laughs), even exist. I was completely against being vulnerable to anyone even my family. I had experience so much exposed and unexposed hurt that being vulnerable to anyone was a no in my mind.

I resisted against relationships and even ruined a few because of my inability to be completely vulnerable out of fear of being hurt. The resistance to being vulnerable somehow gave me a sense of control over my life. Little did I know it was just hardening me even more, but it was being self-inflicted. Being vulnerable also requires you display your feelings and express emotions, everything I had completely shut off to survive the hell I was going through and had been through. Being completely disconnect from my emotions was my go to coping mechanism of survival mode every time. I mean lets really look at vulnerability here, the shit is like learning a completely new language with many unspoken rules and requirements if you're not careful. Learning a new language such as vulnerability can be very daunting, I can attest to that first hand.

Vulnerability, can be the gateway to love. Love is the prequel to healing a heart scared from being held in the hands who couldn't care for their own let alone the delicacy of another. Like vulnerability love is of the components that is needed for an individual (man, woman, or child) to establish peace in one's soul. The soul requires a solid foundation based around love, faith, vulnerability, healing, and forgiveness (in my opinion).

Healing required me to believe in love. Love is the one thing I ran from the most like vulnerability. Love can be the most beautiful thing you have ever laid your eyes on or the most hurtful thing you have ever experienced in your life. Love is what heals the soul after trauma has robbed it of its innocence. Love is the thing most avoided by the broken hearted but long for by them in the same breath. Love is a drug that knows no rehab. Love is what mends a woman's broken pieces when she felt like she was to broken to be loved. Love shows a woman the world is not as cold as she thought once placed in the right hands of serenity. Love is the moment you look into the mirror a realize you are and were love all along. Love is the part of the recipe in life that you cannot skip or the end results will be bitter and bland. Love is me! Love was my rehab from my own pain. Love taught me forgiveness when my mind disagreed. Love has been my teacher and to love I am forever grateful for saving me from bitterness.

Healing challenged me to reach the depths of my soul to understand the importance of forgiveness not only towards others but for myself. Forgiveness to self-first from all the self-defeating thoughts and ideals you impose on yourself is very important. We all have heard the cliché many times that forgiveness of others is not so much form them but for ourselves and our own healing is very true.

Forgiveness is poetry to the heart.

Forgiveness is the line in the sand allowing you to cross to get on the other side of internal happiness.

Forgiveness is freeing once you allow it to become habit and not a chore.

Forgiveness will allow you to fall in love with vulnerability again, feel love, and ultimately allowing yourself to be open to investing in your own healing.

Forgiveness has blessed me in all areas of my life even when I did not feel it was possible.

Forgiveness has allowed me to turn my bitterness into understanding and most of all growth.

Going through this rigorous process of healing required my separation, my ability to get quite with my thoughts, God, and face every fear of what was to come. The boldest thing I could have ever do for myself was face fear head on to become my whole self and come for everything God knew I was meant to be. I had to take a step back from everything and everyone to fully find me the real me through all the hurt. What I discovered was more than finding me but I also found a renewed strength in my relationship with God, faith, love, and my walk with grace that I thought I had lost forever. If you're looking for easy, I can assure you that you are not ready for the process of healing.

Here are a few practical steps I also took in my healing process. Please note that I am not an expert, clinician, or guru. I cannot assure you if you follow same exact steps you will produce the same results.

MY HEALING PROCESS

- I had to first allow myself to cry. For so long I was unable to allow myself to cry as it was a weakness and not a part of cleansing or release of stress. Per WebMD, crying is a natural emotional response to certain feeling, sadness, and hurt. Up until that point I was emotionless and had experienced so much hurt shedding a tear was unnatural to me. By suppressing my tears or ability to feel I was further damaging myself without even knowing it. So, I decided to have a full-on cry fest. I completely broke down and cried my little heart in hopes of releasing any pent-up stress, frustration, hurt, and inability to attach to my feelings.

  Like with the stages in Susanna Barlows article on, "The 5 Stages of Emotional Healing" I had begun to experience: 1. Avoidance, 2. Confrontation, 3. Staying with the Emotions, 4. Clarity and Action, and 5. Epiphany and Gratitude

1. With suppressing my emotions, I was avoiding life all together. I was avoiding any tangible close relationship or friendship with anyone that tried to get close to me
2. I had to confront every emotion I had suppressed, work on building tangible relationships, reestablish

trust, and reach out to my father not matter the outcome.
3. I have and will continue to get in touch with my emotions no matter how hard the process becomes.
4. I have become very adamant about having clarity, being able to hear my own voice, and devise solid plans for my life, and follow-up with action.
5. I have my moments of reflection daily where I would have my epiphany about things, especially when God is trying to get me to recognize a lesson. I try my best to leas with gratitude daily, go to God with gratitude first before I dump my problems upon him, and be grateful for my situation not matter what because there is always a lesson to elevate me.

What does your healing mean to you? And, is it a priority?

_____
_____
_____
_____
_____
_____

Below create a letter to yourself (be open, honest, and forgiving). Speak to the little girl, the woman you are today, and the woman you would like to become. Come back to this letter quarterly and assess your growth. If you have completed some of the things you have challenged yourself to grow from, then create a new one each time.

Bounce Back 6:

What Are Your Pearls?

As I come to the end of my journey with this book, I have experienced every emotion connected to relieving each story. The birth of this book came from the strength in telling my story as I embarked on my relentless self-assessment journey to heal from everything that has plagued my soul up until this very moment.

God reminded me that even though I had been exposed to many storms, death and abuse he was always with me, guiding my steps, and installing the strength that I needed to bounce back from every traumatic moment I experienced. Not every moment in my life was bad or traumatic but for some those moments stick with you the most. So, I decided to face everything that had so much control over me head on.

I had a deep conversation with one of my patients one day. He asked me, what are your pearls, Ebony? I couldn't fully grasp what he was fully asking me at that very moment until I referred to the scripture he had given me which was Mathew 7:6. There was an interpretation that was given: "do not persist in offering what is sacred of value to those who have no appreciation for it, because your gift will not only become contaminated and despised your generous efforts could also be rebuffed, and perhaps even openly attacked." He goes on to explain how important it is to guard your pearls but more importantly to know what your pearls are.

My pearls were, have, and will continue to be delivered to me from each lesson I experience from each trial and tribulation I go through. They have shaped and molded me into the woman I continue to grow to become. My pearls are the keys to my soul, and as I unlock them in hopes of being a blessing to others, I will continue to guard them to prevent them from being contaminated.

The Art of Bouncing Back: How I Survived It All, was birthed from some of the worst moments in my life but blessed me to accomplish some of the greatest accomplishment in my life as well. I was able to turn my pain into purpose!

What are your pearls, queen?

Matthew 7:6 King James Version (KJV)

[6] "Give not that which is holy unto the dogs, neither cast ye pearls before swine, lest they trample them under their feet, and turn again and render you"

(Interpretation) "Do not persist in offering what is sacred or of value to those who have no appreciation for it, because your gift will not only become contaminated and be despised, your generous efforts could also be rebuffed and perhaps even openly attacked."

My Final Thoughts

Inspiration and encouragement is medicine for life's challenges. This medicine will make your world a place of peace and positive thoughts, where you can have your refuge from the stress and strife of the daily grind. Inspiration and encouragement to keep your spirits uplifted when you feel the need to refresh your perspective. Life without life challenges is a faded life, it's where you will gain your wisdom prayerfully.

All of us come across these challenges in life, suffer and then with proper inspiration, prayer, counseling, and encouragement, succeed in the healing process. Explore the most significant challenges of life and also know how to heal them with the help of various therapies and inspiring tools provided. Be open to having real dialogue with your daughter's, your sister's, friends, cousin, aunties, or even the me in your if so the healing process is not forgotten. We are all carrying many pages out of our life that we wish to never recite to the world but not facing them ourselves lies a path of internal destruction.

Life will have various disappointments; some we may recover from and some that will challenge our ability to recover from for the rest of our lives. I lost everything from material possessions, to love, loyalty, friendships, and family but I gained valuable lessons. Being willing to put in the necessary work to **bounce back** no matter what storm approaches brings the strength you never knew you had. The journey has never been easy, I wanted to give up many times, I felt defeated many times, I was depressed, but the main ingredient was that I never ever gave up on me because God never gave up on even when man did. I had to realize just who I was to get back on my walk towards greatness. Even while traveling through valley's in my own life they have been my classroom moments, my healing moments, the opportunity to take great notes, be open to learning, and master listening to God's word for my life. Never be afraid to master ***The Art Of Bouncing Back and Surviving it all***.

About Author

Ebony K. Johnson, is a woman who has experienced life on a multitude of life-changing levels with the ability to bounce back while defying the odds each time.

Ebony is a Registered Respiratory Therapist, received a certification in Polysomnography (sleep therapy), adjunct faculty instructor at a local community college, motivational speaker, and an author who hails from Baltimore, Maryland.

Ebony has always deeply passionate about helping and serving people with philanthropic ambitions. For this purpose, she has pursued such fields of education through which she could attain her goal and ambition of helping while serving others. Ebony holds a double major Bachelor's degree from the Towson University in the fields of Sociology and Anthropology with a focus in criminal justice. Ebony thirst for knowledge and her passion for striving for more and more education assisted her in pursuing her educational career. After acquiring a double major degree, Ebony acquired an Associate of Arts degree from the community college of the Baltimore County in the Respiratory Therapy Program. Additionally, Ebony also holds a certification in Polysomnography Sleep Therapy Program and is currently pursuing a Master's degree in Health Informatics Administration.

Ebony is also an author and a motivational speaker who focuses majorly on spreading the vibes of positivity among the people of the world. Ebony Johnson is also a CEO of Ambitionz R Us which is a platform whose primary objective is to spread positivity, motivate, inspire, and guide individuals. Ebony loves her profession, likes interacting with interesting, and fascinating patients daily.

Ebony realized her purpose after a series of unexpected events, life's trial and tribulations, counseling, and traveling among many valleys. After losing her brother, loved ones, experiencing abusive relationships, sexual assault, abandonment, and learning how to survive it all she has truly mastered *The Art of Bouncing Back*.

To connect with Ebony:

Website: www.ambitionzrus.com

Email: EbonyKJohnson@ambitionzrus.com

Facebook: Ambitionzruseb

Twitter: @AmbitionzRus_EB

Instagram: @AmbitionzRus_EB or @TheArtofBouncingBack

Using Hashtags: #TheArtofBouncingBack or #TurningYourPainIntoPurpose

Made in the USA
Columbia, SC
12 May 2017